D0371925

BRAM STOKER
Author of **Dracula**

BRAM STOKER
Author of Dracula

Nancy Whitelaw

MORGAN
REYNOLDS
Publishing, Inc.

620 South Elm Street, Suite 223
Greensboro, North Carolina 27406
http://www.morganreynolds.com

BRAM STOKER: AUTHOR OF *DRACULA*

Copyright © 2004 by Nancy Whitelaw

All rights reserved.

This book, or parts thereof, may not be reproduced in any form except by written consent of the publisher. For information write: Morgan Reynolds, Inc., 620 S. Elm St., Suite 223 Greensboro, North Carolina 27406 USA

Library of Congress Cataloging-in-Publication Data

Whitelaw, Nancy.
  Bram Stoker : author of Dracula / Nancy Whitelaw.— Rev. ed.
  p. cm. — (World writers)
  Includes bibliographical references and index.
  Summary: A biography of the theatrical manager and prolific author who, among other achievements, completed the novel "Dracula" in 1897.
    ISBN 1-931798-33-8
    1. Stoker, Bram, 1847-1912—Juvenile literature. 2. Novelists, English—19th century—Biography—Juvenile literature. 3. Theatrical   managers—Great Britain— Biography—Juvenile literature. [1. Stoker, Bram, 1847-1912. 2. Authors, English. 3. Theatrical managers.] I.
Title. II. Series.
    PR6037.T617Z95 2004
    823'.8—dc22

                         2003024602

Printed in the United States of America
Revised Edition

$22.00

Young Adult Resources/Bond $

3-23-05

Dedicated to my favorite children's librarian, Camille Guinnane, who serves the children of Chautauqua County, New York with love and dedication.

I gratefully acknowledge the help and encouragement of Barbara Belford, author of Bram Stoker; *David Lass, president of The Bram Stoker Society; Elizabeth Miller, author of* Reflections on Dracula; *Marion Pringle, Senior Librarian, The Shakespeare Birthplace Trust; and Jeanne Keyes Youngson, president of the Count Dracula Fan Club.*

I also thank the researchers at the Library of Congress, the Rosenbach Museum & Library, the Museum of Modern Art, the Romanian Embassy, and The Shakespeare Centre in Stratford-upon-Avon, England.

Property of Dexter
Middle School Library

Contents

Bram Stoker

Chapter One

Imagination Creates a World

When two-year-old Abraham Stoker wanted to go anywhere, he didn't crawl or toddle or walk. He rang a bell. His mother, Charlotte Stoker, would appear, ready to carry him wherever he wanted to go. No one knew why the little boy could not walk. He had been ill since the day he was born, and showed no signs of getting better.

Young Abraham spent most of his time in bed. His family lived in Clontarf, a town on the coast just north of Dublin, Ireland. From his room, he could hear his brother, Thornley, and his sister, Matilda, playing outside. The rumble of trains over the nearby viaduct led his mind along the tracks to faraway places he could only imagine. He listened to the sounds of the wind and the water from Dublin Bay, which was just outside his bedroom window. Sometimes he asked to be seated on his windowsill. There he could watch the tides and the clouds. Once in a while, he saw clipper ships.

His brother Tom was born when Abraham was three years old. Soon his mother was too busy to respond to Abraham's bell. Even when she did, she could not always carry him around. Then his brother Richard was born, and Abraham's bell became even less useful. It was a good day for Abraham when Thornley brought rocks and insects to him, or when Matilda

Charlotte Stoker, Bram's mother.

came to his room to draw pictures with him. The bad days were when the doctor came. He and Abraham's mother talked very quietly about the little boy. Abraham heard worry and fear in their voices. He wondered if he was getting sicker. He wondered if he was going to die.

Because he spent so much time alone, Abraham looked forward to the arrival of meals, to visits from his siblings, and to the regular appearance of his parents to help him with the tasks involved in getting up and then again in going to bed. These rituals were the main contact the boy had with the outside world—besides the dreaded visits from his doctor.

Most of the things young Abraham knew about the world came from the stories his mother told him in the evenings. Some were old Irish tales about characters like

Bram's father, Abraham Stoker.

vampires, who were female bloodsuckers, or Irish fairies that kidnapped children to drink their blood. Abraham loved his mother's stories and begged her to tell more. She could mimic the banshee howl, the wail of a spirit that told of death to come. After a person died, she told her son, his relatives would have to pile stones on top of the grave to keep a vampire from rising. These stones also kept grave robbers out.

Charlotte Stoker knew many stories about starvation, disease, and dying. In the 1840s, later called the Hungry Forties, year after year of crops failed. A fungus attacked the all-important potato crop, further worsening the situation. Abraham's mother vividly remembered the emaciated bodies, rotting corpses, abandoned children, and families torn apart by the potato famine. She even recalled stories of dogs so hungry they attacked and devoured human babies.

The Stoker family had escaped the horror because Abraham's father, also called Abraham Stoker, was a clerk in Parliament, and thus not dependent on harvests for his wages. He had moved his family from the disease-ridden streets of Dublin to the open air of Clontarf, a small town on the city's outskirts. There, young Abraham languished in his third-floor bedroom, alone except for infrequent visits and the company of his imagination. Sitting on his window seat, he told himself stories of storms, shipwrecks, sea rescues, pirates, and unknown lands.

Abraham fed his own imagination with his mother's stories. She described how outlaws were hanged, their bodies left to rot on the gallows. Suicides were buried with stakes in their bodies to keep their spirits from wandering. During the famine, people drank the blood of cows for lack of other nourishment. Cholera was such a deadly and contagious disease that sick people were sometimes buried alive in an effort to stop its spread.

Charlotte Stoker did more for her children than tell them stories. Though she had no formal schooling, she educated herself and passed on a love of learning to her children. Abraham's early learning took place at home with his mother as the teacher and his siblings the other students. His sister Matilda and his brother Thornley helped tutor their younger brothers. Although the family was not rich, they had enough money to buy books, and Abraham read them all.

Abraham's father worked in Dublin Castle. This so-called castle was a group of buildings once used as a fortress and later as a jail. For Abraham, Sr., the job was as uninspiring as the gray stone buildings. Although a faithful worker, he felt unappreciated and bored. He encouraged his sons to look beyond public service for their own careers.

When Abraham was seven years old, he finally began to walk. He was very happy to be able to go outside and play with the other children in his neighborhood. Later in life, he touched lightly on his boyhood illness: "This early weakness passed away, and I grew into a strong boy and in time enlarged to the biggest member of my family." To this day, no one knows the cause of or cure

Abraham Stoker, the year he began to walk.

for his childhood malady. But it is clear he made a full recovery.

Once the boy was able to walk, his father often took him to the theater. After the play, they critiqued each performance as though they were writing reviews. They discussed plots, performances, and scenery in detail. The younger Abraham envied actors because each one could become a soldier, a king, a slave, or any other character that a role demanded. The theater appealed to his imagination.

When he learned to write, Abraham tried to put down on paper some of the stories his mother had told him. He wrote about the cholera epidemic as she had described it to him, and tried his hand at some fairy tales. When he was twelve years old, his parents found the money to send him to a private day school in Dublin run by Reverend William Woods. There he took courses in classic subjects to prepare for college. Although he had only been walking for five years, he took part in athletics eagerly. He pushed his new ability by becoming an endurance walker.

Young Abraham was a very good student, as were his siblings. Most of them went on to professional degrees. Abraham enrolled at Trinity, a highly respected college of the University of Dublin, in 1863. As an invalid child, he had been shy and withdrawn. As a six-foot, two-inch, 175-pound redheaded seventeen-year-old, he was a campus leader. Rugby and football were his favorite sports, and he also swam and rowed. His physical skills earned him several awards for athletics. His ability in the classroom won him awards there, too. He found himself drawn to the poetry of the romantic poets Lord George Gordon Byron, John Keats, and Percy Bysshe Shelley. Though he still lived at home, he spent many nights in pubs around the town, engaged in spirited discussions with his fellow students about these poets and other writers.

In 1865, the elder Abraham Stoker retired from civil service. He had worked in Dublin Castle for almost fifty years but had received little praise and just one promotion. He had gone into debt putting his sons through school. Both Thornley and Richard were already working in medical careers, and this left only Abraham and Tom as students. Young Abraham needed money to fin-

Walt Whitman, the poet who inspired Stoker.

ish his schooling; he took a year's leave of absence to work in Dublin Castle as a clerk. His father was sorry to see his son following in his footsteps, but the younger Abraham was not afraid of giving up his life to work the way his father had. A year later, he was back in school. When he was twenty-one, Stoker first read the poetry of the American writer Walt Whitman. It was a life-changing experience.

Whitman's book of poetry, *Leaves of Grass,* arrived in Europe to a decidedly mixed reaction. On the Trinity campus, students and instructors argued over the work — some thought Whitman was vulgar and disgusting; others praised him as a genius. From his first glimpse into Whitman, Abraham Stoker was a dedicated fan. He thrilled to the lines "Give me now libidinous joys only,/ Give me the drench of my passions, give me life coarse and rank." Some students laughed at Whitman's ebullience and passion, but Stoker took it seriously. He read all of Whitman's work that he could find.

One of the things about Whitman that so appealed to Stoker was Whitman's celebration of male friendships and male platonic love. The word 'homosexual' had not yet entered the vocabulary of Great Britain, and the Victorian era valorized male friendship as the finest and purest kind. Whitman called for his readers to love one another, to reach out to their fellow men, and to celebrate the joys of being alive. Whitman was not afraid of death—he wrote about it as a natural part of life. Stoker was entranced, and defended Whitman's poetry vigorously to anyone who would listen.

Stoker's fascination with words led him to join the Historical Society, a debating group. There, he learned to think and speak quickly. To him, debating was a lot like acting. The debater, like an actor, focused on capturing and keeping the attention of the audience. One of the requirements for belonging to the Historical Society was to present papers to the group. Carrying on the tradition of critiquing plays he and his father had enjoyed, Stoker critiqued literature. Though his father still hoped his namesake would pursue a steady and respectable career, little by little, Abraham Stoker's interests and activities were leading him to the theater.

Chapter Two

The Theater Calls

In 1867, Stoker saw the actor Henry Irving on stage for the first time. Stoker recognized in Irving the same qualities he saw in Whitman—passion for his career, excellence in his performance, and the ability to charm his audiences. Stoker had a new hero. Irving became his role model and idol. Stoker began auditioning for plays— winning a few small parts—and attending as many shows as he could. He continued to go to classes and stay up late discussing and debating literature. It was an exciting time for the young man, and he made the most of it.

In 1871, Irving's performance in the comedy *Two Roses* so enchanted Stoker that he saw the play three times. When he looked in the leading Dublin paper, the *Evening Mail,* he was surprised to see no mention made of the play or Irving's skill. Next he saw Irving star in *The Bells*, the story of a man who commits a murder and gets away with it, only to be forever haunted by the sound of the bells on his victim's sleigh. Again, the *Evening Mail* made no mention of Irving's performance. Stoker was outraged that word was not spreading about the talented young actor, and offered to become drama critic for the paper.

The editor accepted his offer. Stoker received no pay and no by-line. What he did receive was far more important to him—a free ticket to each performance. He became comfortable backstage, chatting with the cast and studying scenery, costumes, and props. Unlike some critics, Stoker always read a play before he saw it. Readers appreciated his reviews because they were witty, honest, and insightful.

Another benefit to this job was that, through it, Stoker became acquainted with Sheridan Le Fanu, joint-owner of the *Evening Mail*. Le Fanu was a popular writer of horror tales. One of his more famous stories, "Carmilla," told of a six-year-old girl who was bitten by a vampire. Stoker enjoyed Le Fanu's gripping tales of nightmares, ghosts, haunted houses, and supernaturalism. Le Fanu wrote in the Gothic tradition, a style of storytelling that highlighted horror stories and other weird tales. Gothic literature became popular in the late eighteenth century, and one reason people enjoyed it was that it allowed them to safely explore their fears. Gothic literature is melodramatic, full of eerie and mysterious events, and thrills its readers with suspense. The stories Charlotte Stoker told her children were in keeping with the Gothic tradition, and Stoker felt immediately at home with Le Fanu's tales.

Twenty-four-year-old Stoker graduated in 1871 with a degree in science and no definite plans for his future. His

Henry Irving, the great actor and longtime friend of Stoker's, as a young man.

father, mother, and sisters had moved to France where Abraham Sr.'s pension would buy them a more comfortable life. His brother Tom was still a student, and his other brothers were busy with medical careers.

Uncertain as to what he would do outside of school, Stoker decided to study for a master's degree in mathematics. He took classes during the day and worked at night to support himself and to pay tuition costs. It seemed natural and easy, although not particularly exciting, for him to return to Dublin Castle as a clerk.

As a young boy, he had dreamed of shipwrecks, pirates, and travel to faraway places. As a college student, he had immersed himself in athletics, debating, and late nights at the pubs. Now as a young man, he could not be content with a desk job that offered no romance, no adventure, and no outlet for his mind and body. The math classes were not sufficient stimulation, nor was his busy schedule of job-related and educational priorities.

Stoker continued to go to plays, read a lot, and work on some short stories he had begun while a full-time student. In 1872, he sold a short story called "The Crystal Cup" to a magazine called *London Society*. He also continued to read Walt Whitman's works. He decided to write to Whitman, and penned almost two thousand words of a rough draft of a letter. At times he was rambunctious, telling Whitman to "put it [the letter] in your fire if you like," then warning him, "but if you do you will miss the pleasure of this next sentence." In other places he was deferential: "You are a true man, and I would like to be one myself, and so I would be towards you as a brother and as a pupil to his master."

Stoker described himself to the poet: "I am ugly but strong and determined and have a large bump over my eyebrows. I have a heavy jaw and a big mouth and thick lips—sensitive nostrils—a snub nose and straight hair." He told Whitman that he was somewhat secretive, even-tempered, and self-controlled, but all this unburdening came to nothing. He put the letter in a desk drawer. Maybe he meant to take it out later and work on it some more. Maybe he thought the letter was pointless since he could not expect to meet Whitman in person. Whatever the reason, he did not mail the letter. Still, he continued to read and re-read his favorite poet's work.

Writing for the *Evening Mail* was a bright spot for Stoker. He continued to study plays in print before he attended performances. He learned about stage lighting and scenery, about casting and directing, and about the impact of dialogue and action scenes. He found friendly faces and interesting conversations among those who worked at the theater.

In addition to making friends and learning the ins and outs of the theater business, Stoker also became a quick and capable writer. Flushed with the excitement of an opening night play, he had to write his criticisms as soon as the curtain closed so his reviews could be printed in the next day's paper. Stoker wrote about more than just the performances. Sometimes he talked about the audience. Once he scolded newspaper readers for not attending a particular play, accusing them of disliking intellectual dramas. Another time he commented on the rowdy audience members who shouted during the play, sympathizing with his readers that it was hard to concentrate on a performance in such situations.

Soon enough, Stoker grew restless working in Dublin Castle by day and spending his nights in the exciting environment of the theater. He wrote to his family and told them that he wanted to give up his civil service career and become a playwright. His father tried to persuade him to stay in the civil service which, he said, was a much more promising career than it had been before. Although Abraham, Sr. admitted that he enjoyed going to performances, he worried that the theater did not have a good reputation. He told his son that it was best to stay away from the class of people who performed on the stage. He went on to say that actresses were little better than prostitutes and that actors were clowns, jesters, and men who would sell their souls for an audience.

His son saw an entirely different picture. But he was in no financial position to leave his steady wages at the Castle, so he continued to live his double life. He consoled himself by writing, and hoped to see more of his work in print. He struggled there, as well. In 1873, Stoker submitted a story, "Jack Hammon's Vote," to three different magazines. Three times, it was rejected. When he sent it to a fourth magazine, he mentioned the previous three rejections in a cover letter and sarcastically challenged them to be the fourth. They rejected him, too.

The next year, he wrote to Whitman again. His prose was more subdued this time, but he told the poet sincerely how his poems had helped him to be more open with people. He mentioned the controversy about Whitman's work and said proudly, "I wage a perpetual war with many friends on your behalf." He also mentioned how much he hoped to meet his hero one day. This time, Stoker did not shove the letter into a desk drawer; he mailed it.

Whitman enjoyed the many letters he got, and returned as much correspondence as he could. He wrote to Stoker, saying, "You did well to write to me so unconventionally, so fresh, so manly, and so affectionately. I too hope (though it is not probable) that we shall one day meet." Stoker was energized by these words, and determined that somehow he would be in the company of his idol.

An eligible bachelor, Stoker went to many parties and dinners. He was tall and graceful, a good dancer known for his waltzing. He made few friends at work, but sometimes went out to taverns with other writers. He lost track of some of his Trinity friends but he did keep in touch with a man named Oscar Wilde who had been a few years behind him. Now Stoker sometimes dined with Oscar and his family. At the Wilde table, Stoker was delighted with the opportunity to talk about science, art, and literature with educated people. Stoker was particularly taken by Oscar's father and his tales of travels in Egypt and other places. He could listen to the older man for hours.

Oscar Wilde would go on to become a famous (and infamous) writer, best known for his novel *The Picture of Dorian Gray* and his play *The Importance of Being*

Earnest. As young men, he and Stoker enjoyed sharing their short story ideas with each other. Stoker's long childhood illness gave him some advantages as a writer. He had probably heard more stories than most children had time for and, in his solitude, he had used his imagination to expand and exaggerate what he heard to increase the mystery, drama, and suspense.

In 1875, three of his stories were published in a popular weekly magazine, *The Shamrock*. They were published in serial form, one chapter at a time. Serialization was popular, especially with readers who could not afford a hardcover book. Sometimes a single story would continue over several years. One especially popular serial writer was Wilkie Collins. His novel, *The Woman in White,* featured a love triangle, a mysterious disease, and an enigmatic woman who might actually be a ghost. This novel had an unusual form: instead of the traditional third- or first-person narration, the story was told in the form of entries from the journal each character kept.

Still studying for his degree at Trinity and working full time at Dublin Castle, Stoker found time to write unsigned editorials for a weekly paper, *The Warder*, owned by his old friend Le Fanu. He also took on an unpaid position with a new daily paper, the *Irish Echo*. There he wrote copy and sold advertising. The *Echo* did not last long because it aimed to be apolitical. *The Warder* was a highly political paper, taking the Protestant/Tory side against the Catholics in Ireland who advocated for Home Rule (which meant they were against being governed by England). Though Stoker's family

Oscar Wilde, Stoker's friend and fellow storyteller.

was Protestant, he was neither very religious nor very politically active. He did come to favor Home Rule, but he generally kept his political opinions to himself.

His father, who had earlier disapproved of Stoker's connections with the theater, now warned his son against connections with a newspaper. He cautioned his son that his association with a politically active newspaper could endanger his position with the government. But Stoker had no intention of staying on at Dublin Castle as long as his father had. In fact, he told his father, he planned to quit his job and move to London to write plays. Again, his father disapproved, warning Stoker that he would not be allowed to get back into government work if his drama career failed—as, he wrote, it probably would.

Stoker's father died in 1876 at the age of seventy-seven. Abraham, Jr. went to Italy for the funeral and then returned to Dublin. Shortly after that, Stoker officially changed his first name to Bram. He was ready to establish himself as his own man.

The same year, Henry Irving returned to Dublin to star in *Hamlet*. Shakespeare's famous play appealed to Stoker because it deals with questions of identity, and forces its central characters to question what is real and what is not. Ghosts and madness haunt the play. Stoker's review praised Irving as Hamlet: "Irving's physical appearance sets him at once above his fellows as no common man." Still, he did not hesitate to identify what he saw as Irving's weaknesses: "the voice lacks power to be strong in some tones, and in moments of passion the speech loses its clearness and becomes somewhat inarticulate."

Irving liked the review, perhaps because of its criticisms, and he invited Stoker to dinner at his hotel. It was the first meeting between the two men, and they became great friends right away. The next night, they dined together again. That evening, Irving stood before Stoker and the other eleven guests to recite the poem "The Dream of Eugene Aram," a story of eccentricity, murder, a corpse that will not stay buried, and a climax in which the murderer confesses and is hanged. Stoker was so moved by the performance that, he said, "I became hysterical." That night, his fate was sealed. He would devote the rest of his life to Henry Irving.

Chapter Three

Art and Business Meet

The friendship between Stoker and Irving continued to grow. Stoker saw as many plays as he could, and Irving was always eager to hear the critic's thoughts. Stoker's visits to the theater kept him busy, but he still found time to court the young Florence Balcombe. Oscar Wilde had been in love with her, as well, but Stoker's attentions were more consistent.

Florence was outgoing and beautiful. Stoker said she was an "exquisitely pretty girl...just seventeen with the most perfectly beautiful face I ever saw." Though Stoker was eleven years older than she, her father approved of the match because Stoker had a secure and promising job. Little did he know the young man had no intention of keeping it.

Stoker had been promoted to Inspector of Petty Sessions, a position that gave him a raise. It also required him to travel for weeks at a time to rural areas. An advantage of the job was that he watched hearings that gave him an excellent picture of the people outside of the cities of Ireland. A disadvantage was that he missed many opening nights in Dublin, and he had to resign his position as drama critic.

Though his job required him only to record the activities of the court session he witnessed, Stoker used the opportunity to study the judicial system. He made extensive notes about what he saw, and researched court documents over the past twenty-five years. Then he wrote a two-hundred-fifty-page long book called *The Duties of Clerks of Petty Sessions in Ireland,* in which he advocated for court reform. He suggested a uniform filing system and a more efficient recording of the collection and distribution of money. Later he described his book as a "complete guide to a clerk's daily duties, from how best to tot up accounts to how to collect fines, deal with dangerous idiots, debts, deserters, trespassing cattle and discovery of arms." The contents reflect Stoker's almost obsessive attention to detail.

In 1877, Stoker had the opportunity to see Irving play Hamlet again. He had nothing but praise for the actor, describing his performance as: "…a wild, fitful, irresolute, mystic, melancholy prince that we know in the play; but given with a sad, picturesque gracefulness which is the actor's special gift."

While Irving was in Dublin, he, Stoker, and other theater lovers frequently dined in restaurants together. Stoker spent a good deal of time with Irving at rehearsals and performances, and chatting with him in his dressing room. He immersed himself in the life of the theater and at the same time, in the life of his hero.

In June, *Vanderdecken* opened, with Irving in the title role. This W. G. Wills play was based on the legend of the Flying Dutchman, the story of Captain Vanderdecken who defied God and therefore was doomed to sail the seas until the Day of Judgment. After the opening night, Stoker and Irving discussed the performance backstage and agreed that the play was too long. They spent the whole night working together to shorten it and found they were very compatible. As Stoker wrote, "We understood each other's nature, needs and ambitions, and had a mutual confidence, each towards the other in our own way, rare amongst men."

Soon after the performance of *Vanderdecken*, Irving became manager of the Lyceum, a fifteen-hundred-seat theater in the middle of London's playhouse district. He sent Stoker a telegram that read, "Will you give up the Civil Service and join me, to take charge of my business as acting-manager?" It was the offer of his dreams: Stoker accepted readily. He resigned his job and in December 1878, he and nineteen-year-old Florence were married in Dublin in a Protestant church. Right after the ceremony, they traveled to London, forgoing a honeymoon so that Stoker could be on hand to help Irving, the man he called the "chief" or "Guv'nor," open a new theater.

The Bram Stokers rented a top-floor flat near a busy market that sold produce, kitchen equipment, and other household supplies. In the dingy neighborhood, street gutters overflowed with sewage and garbage. Pedestrians scurried out of the way when carriages rumbled through the narrow streets. About eighty thousand homeless people slept in unsanitary and unsafe shelters. Although some sewer pipes had been built, most wastewater flowed into the Thames River. Since the river was a source of drinking water, cholera outbreaks were frequent. The city of London was crowded, dirty, and exactly where Stoker wanted to be.

Stoker and Irving threw themselves into the renovation of their new theater. They resolved to make it the finest in London. They agreed to pay actors so well that no one would refuse the offer of a role, and, though the first play was scheduled to open in just two weeks, they decided to completely redo the interior—which they did, incurring a debt of nearly twelve thousand pounds. Stoker took charge of almost every aspect of the changes. He had paid close attention to the theaters of Dublin and knew the importance of color, texture, and lighting. He wanted to create a mood of elegance in his new theater. He also oversaw ticketing, seating arrangements, and publicity. He was excellent at his job, making countless lists and schedules to help keep everything on track and running smoothly.

When opening night finally arrived, Stoker was busier than ever. He checked the box office for last-minute messages, some of which demanded immediate attention. Then he examined all the carpets, drapes, and seats. He checked the orchestra pit for cleanliness and investigated the arrangement of chairs and music stands. He inspected the gaslights. Then he called the ushers to attention and gave them their instructions. He was nervous, but everything seemed to be in order.

Outside the theater, women in long gowns and men in top hats stepped from their horse-drawn cabs. When they entered the foyer, they saw a dramatic scene. Gaslight candles shone on walls and ceilings of blue, green, and gold. Tall red-haired and red-bearded Stoker stood at the top of the staircase, dramatic in black and white formal dress. He personally welcomed each member of the audience. He bowed, smiled, and shook hands with those he knew and those he did not alike. The effect he hoped for had been created: the theater gave off an aura of elegance, and patrons were impressed. The Lyceum was a hit.

The theater season was a whirlwind. As acting manager, Stoker was responsible for overseeing almost every aspect of the productions. Much of his work involved writing letters. Postage for a letter was one penny a half-ounce, and mailmen delivered two and three times a day. Stoker corresponded with actors, suppliers, potential crewmembers, benefactors, and members of the audience. He wrote as many as fifty letters a day and joked: "Fortunately—for both myself and the readers, for I write an extremely bad hand—the bulk of them were short."

Stoker spent time with stage builders, plasterers, painters, and upholsterers, supervising every detail. His attention to minutiae allowed him to make several innovations to theater management. He numbered expensive seats to avoid confusion and to encourage advance booking. In

Oscar Wilde's sketch of Florence Balcombe Stoker.

Property of Dexter
Middle School Library

an effort to build attendance, he advertised performances. And he catered to rich and famous guests by installing the first luxury suite of its kind.

The Lyceum had an old room upstairs that had once hosted the dinner parties of an exclusive club. The club was defunct and the room abandoned, but Stoker saw possibility in it. The room had high ceilings and beautiful wood paneling on the walls. There was an enormous fireplace and room for a long table. Stoker had the room cleaned out and installed a modern kitchen. He bought crystal champagne glasses and decorated the walls with armor and portraits. He and Irving hosted private dinners after performances, and these invitations quickly became the most sought-after in town.

These late night suppers were a gathering of the theater elite. Stoker knew how to cater to his guests, carefully planning everything from the menus to the seating. He and Irving made excellent hosts: Irving was the center of attention, and Stoker made sure all the elements of the evening were in place. As a theater manger, Stoker worked to provide the same kind of predictability and comfort for his guests that he had appreciated as a child who yearned for company and entertainment.

A perfectionist in all aspects of play production, Stoker studied in the British Library, then a part of the British Museum, to create authentic scenery and details. He and Irving agreed that realism was crucial to the success of their plays. They ordered lavish sets, costumes, and props. Irving had to have real food in banquet scenes, real trees and flowers in the scenery, and real gold on crowns and

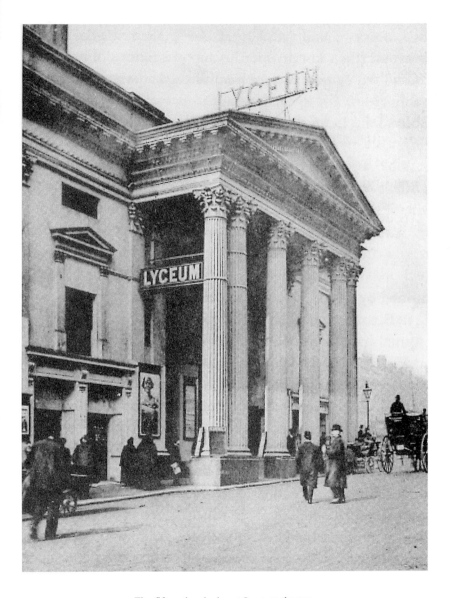

The fifteen-hundred-seat Lyceum theater.

other royal trappings. Irving spent so much that Stoker hid their books lest anyone find out how much money they were pouring into productions.

Irving shared Stoker's attention to detail. During the rehearsal of a scene from *Hamlet* in which Irving, as Hamlet, was to snatch a poison-filled goblet and throw it onto the stage, Irving noticed that when he threw the goblet down, it rolled away. He knew the audience's eyes would follow the goblet and miss the action on the stage. Irving called for the house carpenter and instructed him to alter the goblet so it would not roll. He was not satisfied with the way the poisoned wine splashed out, either, so he experimented with various substances until he decided that sawdust dyed red created exactly the effect he wanted.

The Lyceum was a tremendous success. Stoker was running the hottest theater in town, and Irving was gaining tremendous acclaim as an actor. Stoker was still one of his biggest fans. In 1878, *Vanderdecken* went on stage again, with Irving as the star. Stoker raved about Irving's performance: "[Irving] gave one a wonderful impression of a dead man fictitiously alive." He continued: "[Irving's eyes] seemed to shine like cinders of glowing red from out the marble face." Stoker was mesmerized by Irving, and continued to set aside his own life in order to serve his idol.

Chapter Four

Travels Bring Successes and Trials

In late 1879, the Lyceum scheduled 250 consecutive performances of Shakespeare's *The Merchant of Venice*. The play was hugely popular, largely because of Irving's creation of the character Shylock. A reviewer called the performance "noble and sordid, pathetic and terrifying." Previously, almost every actor had rendered Shylock as a greedy and obsequious letch. Irving saw Shylock differently, and instead of playing Shylock as a disgusting character, he played Shylock upright, as a noble and aristocratic man. Audiences and critics were taken aback by this bold move, but it was successful. The character of Shylock would never be the same.

After the first hundred presentations of the play, Stoker celebrated with a huge party. He invited 350 prominent guests, gave out copies of the play on white parchment paper with gold lettering, and served a seven-course meal.

The Stokers had something to celebrate at home, as

well. On December 31, 1879, Florence gave birth to Irving Noel Thornley Stoker. Bram was thrilled, but little Irving added a complication to his life. Outside of his production duties, Stoker had assumed the responsibility of catering to Henry Irving's every desire. The star believed that he needed Stoker's company each night after a performance to help him unwind and to release the tension that built up on the stage.

In addition to keeping Irving company each night, he was at the actor's beck and call all day. Irving sent messages to Stoker constantly. Many were about insignificant matters, but requiring some action or response. Irving asked Stoker to do an errand for him, to bring him lunch, to invite certain friends to dinner, to remember the color of a cloak they had seen, or any other number of things. On a typical day, Stoker left home in the late morning and stayed at the theater until sunrise. This schedule left little time for a baby. And most importantly, Stoker either would not or could not easily change the relationship he had built up over the years with Irving.

Florence Stoker knew that she could not depend on her husband for help or company. Her husband put Irving's needs first. So Florence took care of herself, making her own friends and social engagements, and enjoying life in London. One constant companion was W.S. Gilbert, one half of the famous Gilbert and Sullivan. When she became nervous or stressed, she took laudanum, an alcohol solution of opium, to calm her nerves, as did many people of the time. The one requirement she made of her husband was that he be home on Sundays, when she usually invited friends to visit. He always complied with this request, and their arrangement suited both of them.

Stoker was completely devoted to Irving, but the actor was a difficult master. He was quick to criticize, and Stoker was often slow to forgive those comments. Irving inspired attention and devotion from a number of people, including many of the actresses of the theater, and Stoker often had to compete with them for his attention. When he had Irving's attention, it was not always in a positive way.

Stoker had always hoped to make something of himself as an actor, and had in fact won a few small parts in Dublin. In 1880, a play at the Lyceum needed several extras in the background of a scene set during a masked ball. A rack of costumes was left in the wings for anyone who felt like filling in that night. One evening, Stoker dressed himself in a large cloak, a mask, and a floppy hat and sidled on stage. By accident, he ended up in the place reserved for the child actors, and, at six feet, two inches tall, stood out quite a bit. Irving thought the whole episode was hilarious, and teased Stoker about it for weeks. Stoker was embarrassed and hurt, and, years later, unable to understand why Irving was so hard on him: "I couldn't myself see anything of a mirthful nature," he wrote.

Perhaps discouraged by his one foray into the limelight, Stoker found time to return to the writing he had done years ago in Dublin. Since he almost never threw anything away, he still had the bits of writing he had done as a boy—fairy tales he had invented, stories his mother

Florence Stoker and her son Irving Noel. In the Victorian age, all children wore dresses, regardless of gender.

had told him, and notes he had made about legends. He found plenty of material for new plots and wrote several stories.

"The Invisible Giant" draws on the stories Stoker's mother told him about the cholera epidemic. The giant of the title is a plague, but only a young girl and an elderly man can see it coming. The story is filled with graphic descriptions of the horrors of the illness, which acts as a moral force, killing all the evildoers of the city. The old man of the story "…knew that the Giant was a very terrible one; and his heart wept for the doomed city where so many would perish in the midst of their sin."

At the age of thirty-five, Stoker published "The Invisible Giant" and seven other stories in his first full-length book, *Under the Sunset.* He dedicated the book to his son. Most of the stories center around the same theme, a battle between good and evil that good always wins. Stoker issued the reader a warning that "the things we do wrong…come back to us with bitterness." The British humor magazine *Punch* called the new work "a charming book," and a *New York Tribune* reviewer said, "the thoughts of the book are high and pure."

1882 was also the year Stoker became a hero. Part of his daily commute was a trip across the Thames River on a ferry. These crossings were generally uneventful, but on one September day, an elderly man jumped off the boat, trying to commit suicide. Stoker reached out to drag him back onto the boat but grasped only his jacket. The man slid out of the coat and plunged into the water, intent on dying. Stoker whisked off his own coat and hat

A newspaper illustration of Stoker's heroic rescue.

and jumped into the river. He swam to the man, grabbed hold of him, and managed to keep him afloat until they could be pulled from the water.

Despite the mouth-to-mouth resuscitation Stoker gave him, the man died on the dock. While some people called Stoker a fool for jumping in since he could have easily been pulled under the boat and drowned himself, the Royal Humane Society gave him

W. S. Gilbert, Florence's society companion.

a medal for his quick and unselfish action. Stoker's name was in all the papers, and for a few days, his fame actually approached that of Irving's.

The Lyceum continued to produce new plays, including *The Cup* by Alfred Tennyson, who later became poet laureate of England. Since Tennyson's play was set in Roman times, Stoker went back to the British Library to do more research. In the library's reading room, Stoker, like other regular patrons, had his own desk, chair, and a peg to hang his hat on. He studied architecture and history so that he could instruct theater workers on the construction of a replica of the famous temple of Artemis—one of the seven wonders of the ancient world. He also helped to design the elaborately embroidered costumes the lead actress and supporting players wore. Reviewers praised the setting as an artistic triumph, although many considered the play less than a dramatic triumph.

Working on *The Cup* gave Stoker the chance to meet Tennyson, a famously reclusive poet. Stoker was in awe of the seventy-year-old Tennyson, but managed to impress him by reciting from his work.

In the 1880s, the Lyceum began touring their productions internationally. Steamships could carry passengers across the Atlantic in less than two weeks, and British actors sometimes traveled to America to perform for audiences there, while American actors occasionally acted in British plays. In 1883, the Lyceum sent Irving, Ellen Terry (one of Irving's favorite actresses), and an entire company to America for a six-month tour. Before the tour, Stoker set up a full schedule of publicity and public relations. He also took care of many personal responsibilities for Irving. He settled the actor's two young sons at school, visited Irving's relatives, and completed necessary correspondence. After saying good-bye to Irving, who sailed on the S.S. *Brittanic,* Stoker settled his own family with Florence's mother in Dublin.

Then he set to work supervising the loading of tons of equipment for twelve plays onto the S.S. *City of Rome.* The equipment included painted scenery, props, calcium lights, and costumes. He arranged schedules, gathered baggage, and fulfilled special requests for about a hundred performers and other people who worked in the theater. When the ship steamed out, Stoker was on his

Tennyson, the most famous poet of the Victorian age.

way to New York. Besides his hopes for successful performances, he had one more desire—while in America, he wanted to meet Walt Whitman.

Once in New York, Stoker was immediately immersed in the business details of the trip—overseeing hotel accommodations; the transportation of props, costumes, and scenery; dealing with reporters; solving personnel problems; and settling conflicts for cast members and workers. It was exhausting work, but Stoker was well prepared to handle it.

The company appeared first at the Star Theater in New York City with a highly praised performance of *The Bells*. Irving starred again as a man who was haunted by the murder he had committed. The company also received high praise for *Hamlet*, which they played in Philadelphia. While their performances succeeded, the troupe's travel arrangements often did not. There were endless delays, and performers were often late for appointments, but through it all, Stoker kept the company together and in good spirits.

Traveling between various cities, the company performed in Detroit, Baltimore, St. Louis, Toronto, Providence, and Cincinnati. American audiences loved the Lyceum actors, and the stars were inundated by invitations to dinners, social clubs, and other entertainments. President Chester Arthur even invited the company to dine at the White House.

One famous American Stoker became acquainted with while in New York City was the writer Mark Twain. They would stroll through the city together, discussing sub-

Henry Irving and the actress Ellen Terry in costume, 1885.

jects of mutual interest, including the roles that nightmares and the subconscious played in their stories. Twain
offered Stoker the opportunity to invest in typesetting
stocks he recommended, and was pleased when Irving
followed suit. Twain told them, "in three years I judge
that this stock will bring fabulous prices." Stoker bought
twenty shares at $50 each, to be paid for on an install-
ment plan. Irving invested five hundred dollars.

Though he was enjoying the trip, Stoker was kept very
busy with work. When the company arrived in Philadelphia, he hoped to get time away to visit his great hero,
Walt Whitman, but was simply too busy. Disappointed,
he sent a note to the writer saying, "If I ever do it [meet
you] it will be one of the greatest pleasures in my life."

Stoker's characteristic obsessions were evident on this
trip. He found out everything he could about America,
and collected as much paperwork as he could. He bought
copies of congressional reports, history books, studies of
the Constitution, schoolbooks, and etiquette books. He
went out of his way to speak to Americans in many
different occupations, quizzing them about their lives
and work as if he was doing research for a play. The trip
was a tremendous success on every level save for one:
Stoker had not come face to face with Whitman.

Chapter Five

Realism Demands Research

One year later, in 1884, the Lyceum made another trip to America, and Stoker's dream was finally realized. Once again in Philadelphia, Stoker took himself away from the company and sought out his literary hero. Whitman was happy to have the visitor, and the men spoke for some time about their correspondence, their writing, and many other aspects of their lives. Stoker later described Whitman as he looked that day: "great shaggy masses of grey-white hair fell over his collar. His moustache was large and thick and fell over his mouth so as to mingle with the top of the mass of the bushy flowing beard." In turn, Whitman wrote of Stoker that he was: "a breath of good, healthy, breezy sea air."

That meeting changed Stoker's life. He decided that now, at age forty, he should make writing a priority in his life. Nine years as stage manger for the Lyceum had shown him that theater work demanded his complete attention. He could not work for the Lyceum and pursue a writing career at the same time. Still, a writing career would not meet his financial needs. He needed a career that would allow him some flexibility in scheduling so he could write. He decided on a career in law.

Stoker enrolled in law classes and was pleased to find that he did not need to attend regularly. To become a lawyer, he needed only to eat in the student hall once during each of the twelve terms and to pass written and oral examinations. The law was not completely new to Stoker. He had learned about court processes while working at Dublin Castle and had learned even more in his research for *Petty Sessions*. Stoker spent more time in the school's library than he did in any actual classes. There, he found it hard to resist working on his fiction, instead of studying law. Despite his busy schedule, he began work on a novel and some short stories. When friends asked why he had chosen law, Stoker joked that it was because lawyers are not asked to sit on juries, and he wanted to avoid jury duty.

Stoker was always working on several projects at once. In 1886, he gathered together the notes he had made in America. These became a lecture and a pamphlet, both called "A Glimpse of America," which he presented in London. True to his predilection for detail, Stoker included such trivia as the fact that America had over 124,000 miles of railroad and that more than 11,000 newspapers and periodicals were published in the country. He criticized the ignorance of Britons about America, saying "[it is] deplorable that we can be left so ignorant of a nation…with whom our manifold interests are not

Walt Whitman as he looked when he and Stoker first met.

Stoker, with his trademark red beard.

only vast, but almost vital." Stoker ended with a plea for mutual understanding: "we are bound each to each by the instinct of a common race." Both his lecture and his pamphlet were well received and Stoker, a behind-the-scenes worker for seven years, now received some applause himself.

As for the Lyceum productions, they continued to be as realistic as possible. Before mounting the play *Faust,* Stoker, Irving, and other members of the company went to Nuremberg, Germany to study buildings and terrain to serve as backdrop to Goethe's scenes. They investigated Nuremberg's old castle and the torture tower. In that tower, they found an Iron Maiden, a cabinet lined with spikes into which a condemned criminal was placed. When the cabinet was closed, the spikes were driven into the prisoner's body and he was left there to die.

Faust was originally a long poem by the German writer Goethe. Faust is a man who sells his soul to Mephistopheles, the devil, in return for magic power and eternal youth. Irving played the part of Mephistopheles. In one scene, Mephistopheles appeared from a cleft in the rocks. Lightning flashed, thunder roared, and the air was filled with inhuman sounds. Witches flew across the stage on broomsticks, and two hundred and fifty war-locks, demons, imps, and goblins pranced and danced on the stage, screeching and howling.

Stoker was particularly proud of the use of electricity in this play. He described how it was harnessed:

> [in this play] two iron plates were screwed upon the stage at a given distance so that at the time of fighting each of the swordsmen would have his right boot on one of the plates…a wire was passed up the clothing of each from the shoe to the outside of the India rubber glove, in the palm of which was a piece of steel. Thus when each held his sword a flash came whenever the swords crossed.

Heating lime (calcuium oxide) on an oxyhydrogen flame resulted in an extremely bright light called lime-light. This light was especially good for pointing to a particular spot on the stage (as with a spotlight), and also to highlight an aspect of a scene or create special effects, such as sunrises and sunsets.

The stories Stoker wrote during this time include "The Squaw," which features a satanic cat. The story is one of his most gruesome. As the hero dies, impaled on spikes in a door, the narrator ends the story by saying: "And sitting on the head of the poor American was the cat, purring loudly as she licked the blood which trickled through the gashed sockets of his eyes. I think no one will call me cruel because I seized one of the old executioners' swords and shore her in two as she sat."

In the fall of 1886, Stoker went to America to make arrangements to show *Faust* in that country. He asked Florence to come with him on the trip. She declined, saying that the trip would be too long and difficult for their son. The couple spent very little time together, but neither seemed to mind. Florence was a popular figure in London society, and Stoker was happy to immerse himself in the world of Irving and the theater.

Stoker paid a second visit to Walt Whitman in Philadelphia. Although Whitman was not well—the poet was nearing seventy and in poor health—he welcomed Stoker. They spent an hour together talking mostly about Abraham Lincoln. Whitman was a great admirer of the president because Lincoln ended the Civil War, which Whitman had been adamantly against. The war went counter to Whitman's belief that mankind should be united by love. When Stoker left, Whitman gave him a copy of his *Memoranda During the War*. It described, among other things, Lincoln's assassination. Stoker's list of personal heroes increased to three—Irving, Whitman, and now Lincoln.

In April 1887, Florence and young Irving Noel survived a disastrous shipwreck. They were adrift for twelve hours before a tugboat rescued them. Still, Florence agreed to go to America with Stoker on the Lyceum tour that year. Aboard the ship, husband and wife experienced opposing emotions. Stoker loved a violent crossing and marvelled at the sea's wild energy. He kept notes of the experience, describing "[clouds] so dank and damp and cold that it needed but little effort of imagination to think that the spirits of those lost at sea were touching their living brethren with the clammy hands of death." In sharp contrast, Florence was frantic with fear throughout the trip. Stoker filled his time on the voyage preparing a lecture about Lincoln, using some of Whitman's work as a resource. He hoped to give the lecture in America.

Once on land, Florence's health and spirits returned. Stoker enjoyed showing her and their son all the sights he was now familiar with. He presented his Lincoln lecture in New York at Chickering Hall on November 25, 1887. While it was well researched, Stoker's talk underestimated the knowledge and appreciation of his audience. A reviewer said it might have been fine for the "ignorant" British, but it fell flat with Americans.

A month later, Stoker made his third visit to see Whitman, whose poetry was as controversial as ever. Stoker tried to convince the poet to edit *Leaves of Grass* so that it would be more acceptable to Victorian society. He begged Whitman to let his friends help with the cutting: "about a hundred lines in all—your books will go into every house in America. Is not that worth the sacrifice?" Absolutely not, answered Whitman: "I think that all that God made is for good—and that the work of His hands is clean in all ways if used as He intended! No, I shall never cut a line so long as I live!" While he wished Whitman's poetry would be appreciated by more readers, Stoker could not help but admire the writer's indomitable spirit.

Chapter Six

Writing Competes with the Theater

When the company returned to England in 1888, Stoker gave his Lincoln lecture, "Abraham Lincoln: How the Statesman of the People Saved the Union, and Abolished Slavery in the Civil War." As the American critic had predicted, the talk was more popular in England than it had been across the ocean. In his lecture, Stoker spoke against the institution of slavery and praised Lincoln.

In the same year, the Lyceum prepared to stage Shakespeare's *Macbeth*, a play about murder, guilt, and ghosts. Many of the scenes in the play take place in a castle, so Stoker, Irving, and other members of the company toured the castles of Scotland, looking for architectural details that would bring reality to the scenes. On this trip, Stoker visited Cruden Bay, a fishing village near Aberdeen on the North Sea. He stayed at an inn called the Kilmarnock Arms and spent his days hiking over cliffs and dunes, enjoying the solitude, wild rabbits, grasses, and flowers. He wandered through the pink

A sketch of the house Stoker rented in Cruden Bay.

granite ruins of three hundred-year-old Slain's Castle. He loved the peaceful views of the small fishermen's cottages, and the fishing nets draped on high poles like a line of black tents. Stoker vowed he would return to the lovely, isolated place.

The Lyceum production of *Macbeth* was well received. Like *Faust, Macbeth* appealed to the nineteenth-century interest in the occult. The publication of Charles Darwin's *Origin of Species,* in 1856, led many people to question their religious beliefs. Darwin's theories about evolution conflicted with religious teachings and many people left their churches or at least reconsidered their beliefs about the origins of life on earth. Darwin's theories were so radical that people began to doubt traditional explanations for many other things, including supernatural events.

Ellen Terry as Lady Macbeth.

The supernatural includes any phenomenon that is thought to be caused by ghosts or spirits, or that is otherwise not easily explainable. While some people became very serious about the supernatural, most of the general public was simply interested in the titillating idea that unknown forces existed in the world. In the mid-1800s, in London, there were at least four publications dedicated exclusively to reporting on supernatural events and attempts at explanations.

People held séances for entertainment and it was quite common to visit fortune-tellers or to have one's palm read. Whether or not people actually believed in clairvoyance or that their future was visible in a crystal ball, spiritualism was a popular fad. Stoker was fascinated by spiritualism, especially as it related to the theater. Attending a play was like entering another realm: one in which magic was possible. Like many of his contemporaries, Stoker was not particularly religious. He wrote, "I often say to myself that the faith which still exists is to be found more often in a theatre than in a church."

Stoker's own interest in the occult led him to a book called *The Land Beyond the Forest: Facts, Figures, and Fancies from Transylvania,* written by Emily Gerard. Gerard was Scottish, but married to an Austrian soldier who was stationed in Romania.

The Land Beyond the Forest was designed to inform its reader about Transylvania, a region in the country of Romania. Transylvania has fertile land, and is notable for the medieval architecture that dominates the landscape. Gerard wrote about the beauty of the country, noting the "indolent charm and the drowsy poetry," and the "strange and incongruous companions" she met there. Stoker was intrigued by Gerard's descriptions of the country, and even more fascinated by an article Gerard published entitled "Transylvanian Superstitions."

The people and customs of the region entranced Gerard. Transylvania is enclosed by mountains and populated mainly by three groups: Hungarians, Germans, and Roma (commonly referred to as Gypsies). The blending of rituals and languages makes Transylvania rich in folktales and lore. Gerard set out to capture these tales in her article, describing ogres, giants, and sorcerers as dramatized by storytellers called *provestitore*. She included material about superstitions revolving around devils, witches, dragons, and vampires. She also wrote about former humans whose penance for their sins was to be transformed into werewolves. Bewitched by the territory, Gerard wrote "it would almost seem as though the whole species of demons, pixies, witches, and hobgoblins, driven from the rest of Europe by the wand of science, had taken refuge within this mountain rampart."

Stoker was fascinated by Romanian customs related to death and dying. He read that some Romanian peasants made their own coffins, and part of the construction process included fitting the future occupant into the burial box to test its size and strength. Family members made a special pillow for the coffin to help the body rest in the grave. Stoker also learned more about *nosferatu*, or vampires.

A vampire is a reanimated corpse. People have believed in the existence of vampires for thousands of years. For instance, Tibetan manuscripts from 2500 B.C tell of blood-sucking creatures with big teeth, and the Irish believed in a blood-sucking monster they called Dearg-dul. Romanians told stories about blood-drinking birds who flew only between sunset and sunrise, and the Mayans worshipped a bat-like god who sucked blood.

Vampires are often described as shape-changers: they can take the form of humans or other animals—wolves, bats, rats, or even mist. Vampires are neither alive nor dead and are often described as the undead. They can only be killed by certain methods, and garlic is reputed to ward them off. Vampires feed on the blood of living people and turn them into vampires, too. Gerard offered instructions for getting rid of them either by driving a stake through the corpse or shooting into the coffin. She also noted that, "In very obstinate cases of vampirism it is recommended to cut off the head, and replace it in the coffin with the mouth filled with garlic…"

To a certain extent, Henry Irving shared Stoker's fascination with things related to death and dying. When the two were in Paris, they often went to the city's morgue, which was open to the public. There, they would examine the bodies that came in, inventing stories about how the person died. Irving brought Stoker with him to court so he could examine the faces of the accused; as an actor, he was very interested in how to communicate emotion. Stoker entertained himself and his friend by telling stories about the prisoners.

Stoker met and became friends with Hall Caine, another writer, who shared Stoker's interest in spiritualism. Caine was six years younger than Stoker, and the author of *The Eternal City*, a novel so popular that it sold a million copies. Like Stoker, Caine was meticulous about research for his novels. In an interview, he told a reporter that he had studied hundreds of volumes in connection with the writing of *The Eternal City*. He too had a family history of storytelling, and he and

Hall Caine

Stoker sat up night after night telling tales of ghosts and other supernatural beings. Caine was also a theater buff and a devoted fan of Henry Irving.

Even on vacation, Stoker continued to do research. In 1890, he took his family to Whitby, a small town of fishermen on the coast of the North Sea in northern England. He spent time exploring and savoring the atmosphere of the town and coastline. Everywhere he went, Stoker made notes—talking to fishermen, studying tombstones in the cemetery, listening to local tales. He studied logbooks and weather manuals, and talked to residents about winds, clouds, and other signs of weather changes.

Whitby is dominated by the ruins of St. Mary's church,

on a hill overlooking the city. One hundred ninety-nine steps lead to the old church and graveyard, where Stoker could look out over the North Sea. He spent a lot of time with sailors, enchanted by their tales of shipwrecks and drownings. A Russian vessel, the *Dimitry,* had wrecked nearby just a few months earlier, and Stoker pored over newspaper accounts of the drama.

Stoker spent many hours in the Whitby library. There he found another book about Transylvania, called *An Account of the Principalities of Wallachia and Moldavia*, by William Wilkinson. He made notes about the land and customs of Romania, using books and maps from the library. Entries from his notebooks such as "Dracula in Wallachian [Wallach is a province in Romania] means devil" show the beginning of what would become his most famous work. He searched for information on the Carpathian Mountains, an extensive European mountain system that ranges through Romania. The wild landscape caught his imagination, as his notes about it show: "Carpathian roads almost impossible in winter, mud, and great stones rolled down on brink of precipice."

He read books about superstitions and legends, books with titles like *Curious Myths of the Middle Ages, The Book of Were-Wolves, The Origin of Primitive Superstitions,* and *History of the Devil.* His notebook was soon full of tidbits about the various creatures he encountered in his reading: "the *penangulam* takes possession of the forms of women, turns them into witches, and compels them to...fly by night to gratify a vampire craving for human blood." Another excerpt from his notebook reports that on the "night before Easter Sunday witches and demons are abroad and hidden treasures then flower." Stoker's imagination was always working, even when he was on vacation.

When Stoker and his family returned to London, he continued to do research on Romania and Romanian customs. He learned that Romanians believed death was only a form of sleep, and that they made holes in their coffins so the dead could hear. He sought out and interviewed Hungarian scholars who could offer more details about the folklore, language, and idioms of the country. Though he never visited Romania, Stoker was soon an expert on the country and its history.

One historical figure stood out dramatically: a fifteenth-century Romanian tyrant known by the names Vlad Dracula, Vlad Tepes, and Vlad the Impaler. His father's name was Dracul, so the son became Dracula. He was called Vlad the Impaler because he reportedly had his enemies impaled on stakes in his garden, and would eat his lunch while watching them bleed to death. Vlad Dracula's story appealed to Stoker's taste for gore.

It is relatively easy to trace the evolution of Stoker's work because he was a pack rat. He kept almost every piece of paper that had writing on it—the flap of an envelope, a piece of stationery, a menu. From these scraps, his fascination with the idea of the undead becomes apparent. He once wrote of a dinner partner: "I sat next to him at supper, and the idea that he was dead was strong on me. I think he had taken some mighty dose of opium, for he moved and spoke like a man in a dream.

A sketch of the bloodthirsty Vlad Dracula.

His eyes, staring out of his white waxen face, seemed hardly the eyes of the living." In another note, he said that an acquaintance looked more dead than alive. In yet another note, Stoker described a friend's laughing face: "[his] upper lip rose and his canine tooth showed its full length like the gleam of a dagger." Sharp canines were typical of vampires, who used them to pierce their victim's skin.

These notes and the copious research Stoker did would eventually add up to become his most famous work, the novel *Dracula*. During the several years he studied and wrote, Stoker also worked on two other novels. The first was *The Snake's Pass*. He called this his outdoor book because he wrote a lot of it outside during August. During this time, Stoker was also accompanying the Lyceum on American tours, and he worked on the book there, as well.

The Snake's Pass is set on the Irish coast, and the main character, like Stoker, feels an almost mystical connection to the sea. The story is typical of Stoker's work in the gothic/horror tradition, involving a disembodied voice, old superstitions, and buried treasure. *The Snake's Pass* was published in serial form in the magazine *The People* and in some newspapers. The book was immediately popular. The other book that occupied his time would eventually be titled *Miss Betty*. Stoker dedicated it to his wife. The book is among his weakest works, with a thin and uninspired story. Though it is meant to be a romantic novel, the story of a woman's faith in the man she loves, Stoker's penchant for the gory is unmistakable: "The red

A modern view of the Romanian castle Vlad Dracula inhabited.

glare of the sunset fell full upon her, smiting her pale face and snowy garments till from head to foot she looked as if dipped in blood." One noteworthy feature of the manuscript is that it contains a scene in which a brave man rescues a person from drowning in the Thames—a clear retelling of Stoker's own experience, though with a happier ending.

Stoker's time in the theater and his background in journalism meant he was able to write quickly and well. He churned out these two novels in hurried snatches, but it would take him years to write his masterpiece. Though he was busy with several projects at once, *Dracula* waited in the wings.

Chapter Seven

Count Dracula Casts His Spell

In 1890, forty-three-year-old Stoker was admitted to the bar after four fairly easy years of study. Though he had planned to become a lawyer in order to support his writing, he found that he was too busy to practice law. His work at the Lyceum took up too much of his time, but Stoker had difficulty leaving the theater. Despite his often-difficult relationship with Henry Irving, Stoker gained enormous satisfaction from his work. He made time for writing when he could.

A year later, Stoker embarked on a venture to bring more literature to more people. He had become a theater critic because he longed to share his excitement about and enthusiasm for the plays he saw. Now, he had a chance to share the books he loved. With the publisher William Heinemann, Stoker founded a line of books called *The English Library.* They bought the rights to work by Henry James, Rudyard Kipling, Arthur Conan Doyle, Hall Caine, and others, and intended to publish smaller, more portable version of these author's works. Unfortunately for them, *The English Library* was in competition with a much older and more established line of almost identical books, and Stoker's business soon folded.

The Lyceum, on the other hand, remained very successful. Stoker's attention to detail continued to help Irving produce the most realistic sets and costumes possible. For an 1892 run of Shakespeare's *Henry VIII*, Stoker sent assistants to a museum to make drawings of tapestry, architecture, jewelry, costumes, and other physical details of the early sixteenth century. Then Stoker and others pored over the drawings, made models, and finally created the stage settings which helped to make *Henry VIII* such a success that it ran for 203 performances.

For all Stoker's seriousness about his work, he also found a good deal of humor in it. One of his favorite stories was about an actor who was supposed to say "cool it with a Dragoon's blood." Somehow, during rehearsals, the words "baboon's blood" kept coming out instead. The actor was beside himself, and vowed to get the line right on stage. But in his nervousness, the actor overcorrected, and, as Stoker loved to report, on the night of the first performance, puzzled audiences watched the man on stage say: "cool it with dragoon's blood—No, no, baboon's. My God! I've said it again! Baboon's blood!"

Stoker also loved the story of another actor whose lines included mention of God's "dwelling place." On stage, the performer forgot the line, and finally ad-libbed: "All shall be well in the immortal land where God hath His—Ah—um—His—apartments."

Though much of Stoker's time and energy was still focused on Irving and the Lyceum, in the snatches of free time he found, he worked on his *Dracula* manuscript. Stoker was a relentless researcher and constantly jotted down notes and ideas on any available scrap of paper— hotel stationery, account book pages, old letters.

He decided to set many scenes in Styria, a region in Austria. Using the myriad notes he had, Stoker was able to create a working outline. Despite his methodical research, his ideas seemed to come in flashes. The notes he made are often just fragments, enough to capture an impression he could return to later: "the journey—wolves howl and surround—blue flames—driver stops—knife thrown and strange sounds." He made a list of characters: a lawyer's clerk, a mad doctor, a mad patient, a girl who will die in the story, and, of course, the count who would become Dracula. He also made notes to ask his brother Thornley, a surgeon, questions about injuries that cause comas or death. The plot of his most famous novel was gradually unfolding.

In 1893, Stoker's work was interrupted by a lucrative job offer. The artist J. McNeill Whistler, later famous for his painting of his mother, asked Stoker to handle his financial affairs for him: "I really think it would be worth a good man's while...I would give half of all I earned to such a man," he said. Stoker was intrigued by the offer, but had to refuse it. He could not take on Whistler without abandoning either Irving or his writing, and he

Henry Irving and Stoker leaving the Lyceum. Irving is on the left and Stoker on the right, as always, following his hero.

did not want to give up either.

On what was becoming a yearly vacation to Cruden Bay, Stoker wrote a short story called "The Watter's Mou" ("The Water's Mouth"), which focused on places and people he met in Cruden. The story is a tragedy involving smuggling, but it stays true to Stoker's macabre tastes. One passage describes a boatman looking down into the sea and spying "a mass that in the gloom of the evening and the storm looked like a tangle of wreckage—spar and sail and rope—twirling in the rushing water round a dead woman, whose white face was set in an aureole of floating hair."

Encouraged by how well his writing was going, Stoker polished up *Miss Betty* and sent the manuscript to a publisher. At forty-seven, Stoker wanted to be able to give up his exhausting duties at the theater in order to write full time. But he could not afford to do so unless his writing sold. The publisher rejected *Miss Betty*, saying it did not have a strong enough plot. Stoker was disappointed to think he could not make a living as a writer after all. He had a family to support, and resigned himself to staying at the theater.

Life at the Lyceum proved to be as exciting and eventful as ever. For Cervantes' play *Don Quixote*, Stoker was in charge of procuring a broken down old nag for Irving to ride as Quixote. On the day of the first performance, Stoker went to pick up the horse only to find its owner had been fined for cruelty to animals, and the starving animal had been shot. Only hours before curtain time, Stoker had to find a suitably impoverished-looking creature to carry Irving on stage. At the last minute, he solved the dilemma by hiring a horse used to pull a hansom cab. This animal was beautifully groomed and well-fed, so for each performance its mane was tousled and its sides painted to simulate prominent ribs.

The Lyceum had one of its few failures with *Madame Sans-Gene*, a play about a father who severely mistreats his son. The story was brutal and shocking, and when a tortured body appeared on stage, bloody and beaten, several audience members fled the theater. Others protested that the Lyceum had gone too far in its zeal for realism. Stoker defended the play, saying: "The history of the time lent itself to horrors," but word quickly spread. Ticket sales dropped. Stoker and Irving revised the play to cut the most gruesome scenes, but after a month of nearly empty houses, the play had to be closed.

While the Lyceum could have rebounded from a poorly received piece, the company's financial woes were beginning to add up. In an attempt to save money, the usually extravagant Irving persuaded Stoker to reduce the insurance coverage on the property—which was already underinsured. While the move kept the Lyceum solvent, it would prove to be a mistake.

The notes Stoker made for *Dracula* during this time show the story continuing to develop and cohere. He named his characters: the hero, a lawyer's clerk, became Jonathan Harker; the mad doctor was Dr. Seward; the mad patient, Renfield; the girl who dies, Lucy Westenra. He first called his villain Count Wampyr, a Slavic spelling of *vampyr* and the foundation for our present word *vampire*. Then he changed the name from Count Wampyr to Count Dracula. Sometimes in his notes, he called him simply Drac. He changed the location of main scenes from Styria to Transylvania, Romania. His notes at this time begin to look increasingly like the outline for a book. He filled in names and sketched in scenes noting the dates, and sometimes the times, of each event. He made brief but specific notations: "Aug. 11. bat outside Lucy's window"; "July 4. Jonathan at hospital."

One of the reasons *Dracula* would become hugely popular when it was published was the general popularity of anything having to do with mysticism or the occult. Victorian England was fascinated by stories of supernatural events or experiences; hypnotism, tarot readings, and phrenology were all the rage. Stoker's old school friend, Oscar Wilde, was married to a woman named Constance who was a devoted follower of mysticism. Stoker gained much of his knowledge of tarot from her. Tarot cards are illustrated with characters who represent various aspects of man and nature. Believers claim they can tell the future by the order in which a person draws the cards.

Hypnotists were popular at parties, where they would put people into trances. Oscar Wilde's most famous book, *The Picture of Dorian Gray,* features a kind of hypnotism. In the novel, Wilde pushed Victorian readers beyond their limits with thinly veiled allusions to homosexuality. Wilde himself was eventually tried and convicted for engaging in homosexual acts. Wilde served two years' hard labor in a British prison before he was released. An outcast upon his release, Wilde lived the rest of his life in France under a pseudonym. His story and his trial were all over the newspapers at the time, and though Stoker was at times close to Wilde and his family, history does not tell us whether Stoker supported his old friend. There is an undocumented story that claims Stoker visited the self-exiled Wilde in France, bringing him money, but we have no proof of the story's truth.

Wilde was castigated for the air of homosexuality that pervaded his novel, even if the relationship was never explicitly named. Later, readers would find reason to see homosexual references in Stoker's *Dracula,* too. Stoker escaped criticism, though, likely because the macabre nature of his novel obscured any homosexual interpretations of it.

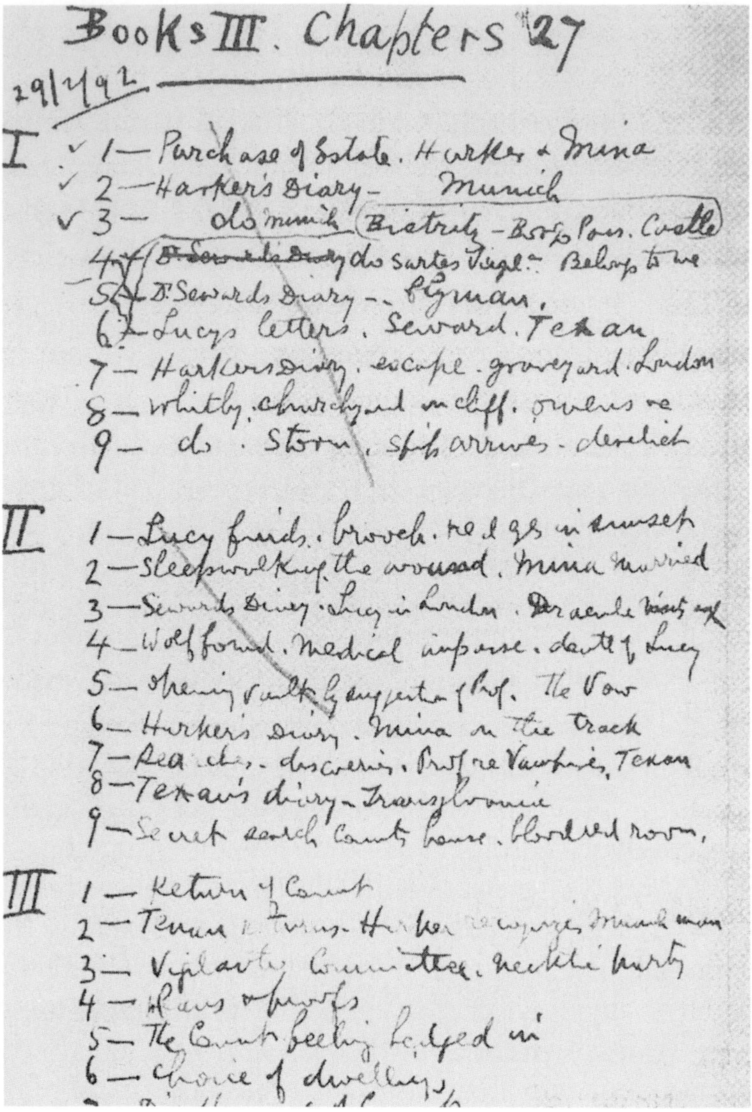

Books III. Chapters 27

29/2/92

I ✓ 1—Purchase of Estate. Harker & Mina
✓ 2—Harker's Diary— Munich
✓ 3— ~~do Munich~~ (Bistritz—Borgo Pass. Castle)
4 ~~[illegible]~~ do Sortes Virgil— Belongs to me
5 Dr Seward's Diary— Flyman.
6 Lucy's letters. Seward. Texan
7— Harkers Diary. escape. graveyard. London
8— Whitby. churchyard on cliff. [illegible]
9— do. Storm. Ship arrives—derelict

II 1—Lucy finds. brooch. [illegible]
2—Sleepwalking the wound. Mina married
3—Seward's Diary. Lucy in London. Dracula [illegible]
4—Wolf found. Medical [illegible]. death of Lucy
5—Opening vault by suggestion of Prof. The Vow
6—Harker's diary. Mina on the track
7—Searches. discoveries. Prof re Vampires, Texan
8—Texan's diary—Transylvania
9—Secret search Count's house. blood red room.

III 1— Return of Count
2— Texan returns. Harker recognizes Munich man
3— Vigilante Committee. necktie party
4— Plans & proofs
5— The Count feeling hedged in
6— Choice of dwellings,

A page from Stoker's notes for his novel *Dracula.*

The plot of *Dracula* revolves around a young real-estate agent, Jonathan Harker, who is sent to Transylvania to complete a sale of land to Count Dracula. Harker has no reason to fear Dracula, until he arrives at the count's castle and slowly realizes that Dracula is a vampire who is buying property in England in order to spread vampirism there. While Stoker did not invent the idea of the vampire, he did bring it to the forefront of public attention. The vampire has proved to have tremendous staying power. Literally hundreds of movies have been made featuring vampires, and vampires have become fixtures in horror novels and stories around the world.

One of the reasons *Dracula* is special is its form. Perhaps borrowing from Collins and his popular novel *The Woman in White,* Stoker decided to write his book almost completely in the form of letters and diaries written by various characters. One such journal entry records Jonathon Harker's confusion when he discovers that the count has no reflection. Harker has been sent from his lawyer's to visit the reclusive count (no one yet knows he is a vampire) and bring him some paperwork. The count is a cordial host, and invites Harker to spend the night in his castle. The next day, Harker writes in his journal, that, while he was looking in the mirror to shave, "suddenly I felt a hand on my shoulder, and heard the Count's voice saying to me, 'Good morning.' I started, for it amazed me that I had not seen him, since the reflection of the glass covered the whole room behind me...I turned to the glass again to see how I had been mistaken...there was no reflection of him in the mirror."

Readers knew that one sure sign of a vampire is that the person has no reflection.

Dracula is filled with the horror writing Stoker so enjoyed. Part of the plot concerns a doctor, Dr. Seward, and his mad patient Renfield. In a typical diary entry, Dr. Seward wrote about Renfield: "He disgusted me much while with him, for when a horrid blow-fly, bloated with some carrion food, buzzed into the room, he caught it, held it exultantly for a few moments between his finger and thumb, and, before I knew what he was going to do, put it in his mouth and ate it. He argued quietly that it was very good and very wholesome."

The only exceptions to the letter and journal style of the novel are the scenes in which Count Dracula speaks. In those scenes, Stoker writes in dialogue, recording the count's words as he speaks them, not as another character remembers them. To Jonathon Harker, the count says sweetly: "You may go anywhere you wish in the castle, except where the doors are locked, where of course you will not wish to go. There is a reason that all things are as they are."

As a finishing touch, Stoker dedicated the book to Hall Caine, calling him Hommy-Beg, a loving nickname given to Caine by his grandmother. The novel took more than seven years to complete and stands above his work at the Lyceum and his numerous other stories and novels, as his greatest legacy.

Chapter Eight

A Writing Career Flourishes

On the morning of May 18, 1897, posters went up outside the Lyceum. They announced that the theater would hold a reading of Bram Stoker's latest work. Such reading of a yet-to-be-published manuscript served as an official request for copyright on the material. Fifteen Lyceum company actors took various parts for the four-hour reading. A small audience of crewmembers, performers, and a few passers-by listened. Two days after the reading, Stoker decided on a title, rejecting *The Undead* in favor of the shorter, more dramatic and exotic, *Dracula*.

Stoker's dream was to produce the story as a play with Henry Irving as Dracula. He submitted the manuscript to the Lord Chamberlain's office where a reader declared that it was morally fit to be performed on stage, and granted it License #162. However, when Stoker asked Irving what he thought of the manuscript, Irving answered with just one word—"Dreadful!" Stoker immediately abandoned any plan to stage his novel.

Two weeks after the reading, Stoker waited anxiously at a nearby bookstore for the first copies of his new book to arrive. He hoped that the published book might wear a red jacket with gilt letters highlighting his name and the title. He was disappointed to find the books were not bright red, and there was no gold on the cover at all. Instead, the novel was wrapped in a cheap yellow cloth cover, and the red letters *Dracula* by Bram Stoker hardly caught the eye. Despondent, Stoker wondered how many of the three thousand published copies would sell.

Stoker did everything he could think of to increase sales of his book. He pressured reviewers to write about it. He had boxed, leather-bound copies made for his important friends, such as British Prime Minister William Gladstone, who was determined to rescue Ireland from centuries of British domination. He and Stoker had established a friendship in part because of their mutual support for an independent Ireland. With Gladstone's gift copy, Stoker sent a note: "the book is necessarily full of horrors and terrors, but I trust these are calculated to cleanse the mind by pity and terror." Stoker sent another five hundred copies to other acquaintances and hoped to increase sales through word of mouth.

Charlotte Stoker, who had been the source of so much of her son's thirst for stories and storytelling, read the book and wrote to her son: "My dear, it is splendid." She praised the terror of the novel and promised Stoker the book would make him rich. Reviewers offered differing opinions. *The Athenaeum* said the book "reads at times

The cover of a 1901 reprint of *Dracula.*

like a mere series of grotesquely incredible events." A reviewer for the *Pall Mall Gazette* wrote: "It is excellent. One of the best things in the supernatural line." The *Daily Mail* called it a "weird, powerful and horrible story." One reviewer asked how Stoker dared to describe Romania since he had never been there. Stoker answered: "Trees are trees, mountains, are generally speaking, mountains, no matter in what country you find them, and one description may be made to answer for all."

Despite Stoker's efforts to create publicity, the book was not a hit. Part of the reason for poor sales was that Romantic novels were out of fashion. In 1848, almost fifty years before *Dracula,* three artists, Dante Gabriel Rossetti, John Everett Millais and William Holman Hunt, joined together to form a society they called the Pre-Raphaelite Brotherhood. The society was named to honor the Renaissance painter Raphael. Rossetti and his compatriots formed their society as a protest against the type of art popular at the time, which they saw as artificial and unworthy. The Pre-Raphaelites called for a return to realism, to art that was true to nature, and to subjects worthy of preservation for the ages.

By the end of the nineteenth century, British literature had turned away from the Romantic style and was focused more on realism and the lives of actual people. The Victorian era saw a fascination with progress, and an increasing awareness of the markers and dividers of class and wealth. Had *Dracula* been published during the Romantic era, sales might have been better. But Stoker's latest book was simply too late. It seemed old-fashioned and out-of-date. *Dracula* would grow in fame and fortune over the years—but Stoker would not live to see it happen.

In February 1898, a fire destroyed the storage area of the Lyceum. Costumes, scenery, and other stage properties for forty-four plays went up in flames. The loss was enormous. Because Irving and Stoker had reduced their fire insurance, the company was suddenly without almost everything it needed to stage plays, and had hardly any money at all with which to rebuild. Irving was bedridden with pneumonia, and Stoker scrambled to recover whatever was salvageable and to create new props and scenery as necessary for the immediate future.

As Stoker hurried to rebuild the Lyceum's sets and to reassure theatergoers that the company would be back on its feet, Joe Comyns Carr, a leader in the cultural circles of England, visited Henry Irving in his sickroom. Carr was keenly interested in the Lyceum, and outlined to Irving a plan whereby a syndicate would take over the theater and the company. Depressed and ill, Irving agreed. Under the conditions of the takeover, Irving would continue as actor-manager of the theater, would give one hundred performances each year, and would receive a cash settlement.

Stoker was boarding a ship to America, on his way to another tour with the Lyceum company, when he heard the news. He was hurt and angry that Irving had not consulted him before turning over the theater that he had managed for almost twenty years. Though he was troubled by Irving's decision, Stoker never said a word. He carried

Mark Twain with his daughter Clara in London.

on with his commitments as if nothing had changed. In some ways, Harker's relationship with Dracula is reminiscent of Stoker's relationship with Irving. Irving occupied Stoker's life in much the same way that Harker is dominated by the vampire count. Dracula and Irving both represent a charismatic force that no amount of protest could halt.

When Stoker and company returned to London, Stoker was invited to write a sketch about himself for *Who's Who*. This honor meant his name was recognized as one of the most important in the city. In filling out the form for the entry, he found a blank after the word "Recreations." He filled in "pretty much the same as the other children of Adam." This clever reply was an allusion to a poem of Whitman's, in which the children of Adam are fun-loving, active, and clear-headed youth.

That year, Mark Twain came to London. Twain's venture in typesetting stocks had failed, and feeling obligated, he made up both Stoker's and Irving's investments out of his own pocket. In London, he asked Stoker to be his agent. Twain hoped to sell his adaptation of a German play to English audiences. Although the idea did not work out, the two men renewed their friendship and enjoyed many hours of conversation.

The same year, Stoker found a publisher for *Miss Betty*. Though several turned it down, when it finally came out, the reviews were good. But after the difficulty of *Miss Betty* and the challenge of seven years with *Dracula*, Stoker settled into writing short stories. His work habits—jotting down a sentence here and there, and pages and pages when he was more inspired and had more time—were perhaps better suited to short works than long ones.

Stoker continued to write grotesque and macabre tales. In "The Squaw," he created a richly detailed torture tower, which had swords designed specifically for beheading, chairs full of nails, and the Iron Maiden torture device he had first seen in Nuremberg. In "The Burial of the Rats," the narrator is fleeing through the slums of Paris when he trips: "Splash! My feet had given way in a mass of slimy rubbish, and I had fallen headlong into a reeking, stagnant pool. The water and the mud in which my arms sank up to the elbows was filthy and nauseous beyond description, and in the suddenness of my fall I had actually swallowed some of the filthy stuff."

In 1899, the publishers Doubleday & McClure announced the first American edition of *Dracula*. For some reason, Stoker applied for American copyrights on his work, but never sent in the two copies of the book that would have completed his application. Since Stoker did not own the rights to his work in that country, he was never paid for its use there. The story was serialized in newspapers in the States and had some popularity, but not until the silent film *Nosferatu,* made in Germany in 1922, did the Dracula story boom overseas.

Stoker made his sixth trip to America in the same year. With the Lyceum company aboard, the ship sailed into the most violent weather Stoker had ever seen. It was a hurricane with winds up to one hundred miles an hour— a strange storm without any rain. While the rest of the

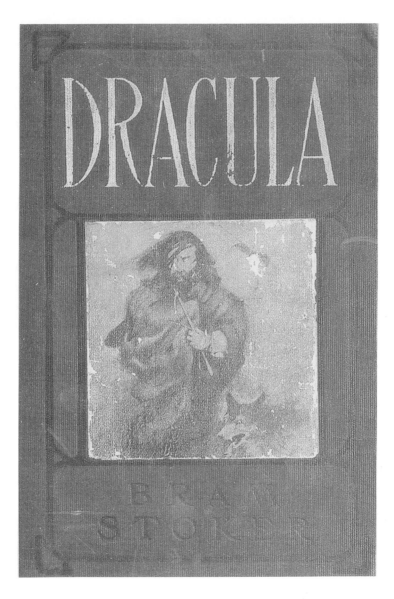

The cover of the first American printing of *Dracula.*

passengers and crew huddled in their berths, Stoker stood at the rail, marveling at the mountainous waves and the wind roaring like a banshee. Stoker described the weather as so fierce that "at times we rolled so that our feet shot off the deck." Fastened-down trunks strained at their ropes until they broke away. Stoker earned a deep gash in his leg trying to catch and refasten them.

Once the company arrived in America, Stoker was elated to discover that he was no longer known just as Irving's valet. He was famous now on his own—as the author of the much-talked-about *Dracula*. One reviewer seemed surprised that the writer of the latest horror novel was: "a great shambling, good-natured overgrown boy...with a red beard, untrimmed, and a ruddy complexion tempered somewhat by the wide-open full grey eyes that gaze so frankly into yours. Why it is hard to imagine Bram Stoker a business manager, to say nothing of his possessing an imagination capable of projecting *Dracula* upon paper."

When the Lyceum players returned to London, it was to a city that was rapidly becoming internationalized. City dwellers now had new and efficient sewers and water pipes, large stores, a subway, a telegraph cable, higher standards of living for workers, and a flurry of new magazines and newspapers. Competition among theaters increased. When Irving had taken over the Lyceum in 1878, it was one of just seven city playhouses performing dramas. By 1900, there were more than twice that many theaters competing for the attention of theatergoers, and there was a tremendous variety of shows to be seen.

As London continued to grow, city planners issued new safety regulations for public buildings. The Lyceum was in an older building and would have required expensive repairs to be brought into compliance. The decision was made to sell the theater rather than try to cope with the additional expenses. In 1902, Irving gave his last performance on his beloved stage. Stoker and Irving arranged an enormous party for the last night of

A contemporary sketch of Bram Stoker.

drama at the Lyceum. After the curtain closed, the stage was quickly refitted with gorgeous draperies, thousands of flowers, and elaborate decorations. The curtains were reopened and the audience members were invited on stage to eat, drink, and celebrate the memory of the most fashionable theater in London.

While his career at the Lyceum was ending, Stoker also lost his greatest champion, his mother. Charlotte Stoker died in 1902 at the age of eighty-three. Her loss added another weight to Stoker's shoulders. In the past two years, Oscar Wilde had died, in exile, still in love with Florence Stoker, and the rein of Queen Victoria had ended with that monarch's death. A new era was beginning.

Irving, Stoker, and the rest of the company made one more American tour. The trip did not go well. Audiences were small, and expenses were high. Though the trip did turn a small profit, its greatest success was offering Irving and Stoker an excuse to avoid being present for the auctioning off of the contents of the Lyceum.

When they returned to England, Irving was still weak from his recent illness, and despondent at the closing of his theater. He stopped going out in public, and invited only select friends to his apartment. Stoker was not one of them. Their friendship stalled, and Stoker was left with neither a job nor the friend he had so long served. At the age of fifty-six, he hoped to find work as manager of another theater, but no one was interested: he was a relic.

Though Stoker made an effort to keep his name in the public eye, no jobs were offered and he spent most of his time writing. He finished "The Secret of the Growing Gold," one of his most macabre tales about a murdered woman whose golden hair grows out of the flagstones under which she is buried. He set a goal of writing a book a year. He returned to Cruden Bay where he studied Scottish history, witchcraft, and second sight. He lay in a hammock, surrounded by the sounds of the sea, and there he wrote *Mystery of the Sea*. This novel revolves around the discovery of a great sunken treasure. The book uses a first person narrator, and includes scenes of madness, and violence. Stoker hoped to have *Mystery of the Sea* performed on the stage and adapted it into a five-act play himself.

He spent hours in the library, researching Egyptian

history to write *The Jewel of the Seven Stars*, a novel about an Egyptian queen's wish for resurrection. This 1903 book is full of fantasy, dreams, and nightmares. Its mysteries include a strange birthmark, a seven-clawed creature, a ruby that might have supernatural powers, and experiments in the occult. In 1904 he completed another novel, *The Man*. The central character is a woman named Stephen who exemplifies the plight of women at the turn of the century. Because she is a woman, Stephen finds herself unable to speak her true feelings and lives most of her life in love with someone but unable to tell him so— the rules of their society prevent her. Neither book was particularly well received. Stoker's literary star seemed to be dimming.

Chapter Nine

Goodbyes

Henry Irving never fully recovered from his bout of pneumonia. In 1904, he and Stoker reunited for a farewell tour in some of the smaller theaters outside of London, but it was a doomed effort. Irving could barely walk and was short of breath. He managed to take the stage for a few performances, but each one left him weaker. Finally, Stoker had to suggest to his old friend that they cut their schedule short. Irving had hoped to make one final trip to America, but had to accept he was too sick.

Irving gave his last performance as Becket in the play of the same name. After the show, he came out from behind the curtain and thanked the audience for their support. Backstage, he said goodnight to Stoker, uncharacteristically clasping his hand, and then the two men parted ways. A few hours later, Irving collapsed and died in the lobby of his apartment building.

All of London mourned Irving's death. Flags were

lowered to half-mast, and black ribbons adorned every theater in the city. Irving was the first actor ever to be knighted, and his funeral was befitting. He was cremated and his ashes interned in Poets' Corner of Westminster Abbey, the first actor to occupy that hallowed ground. He joined monuments to such luminaries as Tennyson, John Dryden, Shakespeare, Geoffrey Chaucer, John Milton, Keats, and Shelley.

Irving's death was very difficult for Stoker, who had so long devoted himself to the man. Public sympathy went to Stoker's side, which was fortunate for him since neither his wife nor his son joined him in mourning. Florence Stoker had, for her entire married life, shared her husband with another man. Their son was named Irving but as an adult, he refused to answer to it and began to call himself Noel, his middle name, so as not to honor the man who stole his father. Irving's death was a hard blow for Stoker, and he bore it alone.

A year after Irving's death, Stoker published a glowing memoir called *Personal Reminiscences of Henry Irving*. Using old journal entries and the many notes he had made over the years, he put together a series of stories portraying Irving as a fine artist who had made the most of his talents. Stoker thoroughly admired Irving and was clearly proud of the role he had played in the artist's life. Even though Irving was dead, Stoker could not resist the urge to thrust him into the spotlight again, and to broadcast far and wide the news of such a talented actor. Stoker followed the success of this book with a series of lecture tours in which he regaled audiences with stories and anecdotes about his idol.

Stoker went back to theater management one last time. He was acting manager for a West End musical production of Oliver Goldsmith's *The Vicar of Wakefield*, a story of the misfortunes of a clergyman and his family. The play closed in just two months. After that, Stoker never stayed long on one project. He organized a theatrical exhibition, took part in the Dramatic Debaters (as eagerly as he had debated at Trinity), and became active in a writers' society. He wrote a series of articles on cultural trends covering subjects as varied as American actors, censorship, and the possibility of building a national theater

Then, in 1906, Stoker suffered a stroke. His eyesight and his ability to walk were permanently impaired, and he needed a magnifying glass to help him read and write. His whole body was weakened, and he was frequently bedridden. Florence cared for him, much as his mother had done when he was a child.

Dracula still earned royalties, but the money was not enough to provide a living for Stoker and his family. To make ends meet, he returned to journalism and served for a short time as a writer for the *Daily Telegraph*. He wrote some profiles for the *New York World*, including one of Winston Churchill, who later became prime minister of England.

Stoker also joined the controversy raging over censorship in England. He wrote articles urging book and newspaper publishers to refuse to print "unclean" books and the "foully-conceived novel." In an article for *Nine-*

teenth Century, he said: "A number of books have been published in England that would be a disgrace to any country…the evil is a grave and dangerous one."

The books Stoker referred to were graphically sexual. He and others worried that the more permissive Edwardian era (Edward VII replaced Victoria at the throne) would allow the publication of what they considered to be lewd fiction. In his youth, Stoker had defended Whitman's poetry, also considered obscene in its time. But, in Stoker's opinion, these new books really did go too far. While *Dracula* is inarguably erotic, its sensuality was somewhat disguised by the supernatural elements of the plot. Nearly twenty-five years later, an Irish actor, Hamilton Deane, would try to adapt Stoker's novel for the stage. When he submitted a script to the Lord Chamberlain's office, he found that censors would not approve what they called a disgusting story. Not until *Dracula* was substantially altered to be more comical than horrific was the production approved.

In 1908, Stoker worked on two books at once: a work of fiction, *The Lady of the Shroud,* and one of nonfiction, called *Famous Imposters. The Lady of the Shroud* returns to Stoker's fascination with the occult, and is also written mostly in the form of letters. Stoker used material he had learned from Romanian legends and tales to create dark and terrifying scenes with vampires and coffins. He also used the knowledge he had learned studying the law to write convincingly about wills and other related subjects, including codicils, testators, and witnesses.

Some people found it hard to imagine that a man so apparently ordinary could have written *Dracula.*

In *Famous Imposters*, Stoker opens with the asssertion that "imposters in one shape or another are likely to flourish as long as human nature remains what it is." This book is an unusual departure from the rest of his work because it is nonfiction. In it, Stoker puts forth some rather strange theories, including his speculation that the never-married Queen Elizabeth had actually been a man.

Stoker's health continued to decline. Florence was by his side night and day, and they were happy to see their son Noel, now an accountant, married. Stoker followed the typical regimen for his problem—a little arsenic, strong soups, and no meat. Stoker's health was not the worst of it; their finances were of gravest concern. Several times, Stoker wrote letters to his brother Thornley in which he indirectly pleaded for money and also described his ill health: "I can now stand for a few seconds at a time on the one leg and better still I am able to work, the book [*Famous Imposters*] is getting on...Anyway happy memories are all anyone can ask for."

Thornley never came through with any money for his younger brother, and in February 1911 Stoker had to ask the Royal Literary Fund for help. The Fund was set up to help writers who were unable to make ends meet, and required the applicant to provide proof of impoverishment in order to be eligible for assistance. Several friends wrote on Stoker's behalf, and the Fund awarded him one hundred pounds—the most it ever gave. Despite this help, he and Florence were forced to move into smaller quarters even as Stoker's health continued to fail.

In March, Stoker began writing *The Lair of the White*

Worm. He wrote with a sense of urgency, aware that he did not have much time. He took to dating each day's work, something he had never done before, and finished the novel in less than four months. The book, his eighteenth, concerns a two-thousand-year-old giant white worm named Lady Arabella who is wreaking havoc all over the Yorkshire countryside. The hero of the novel has to find a way to destroy her lair, which he finally does with dynamite. The novel is choppy and confusing and yet was Stoker's most popular work, after *Dracula.*

Ten months after he finished *The Lair of the White Worm,* Bram Stoker died. On April 20, 1912, at the age of sixty-four, Stoker was pronounced dead from kidney problems and other complications, including exhaustion. While exhaustion was not a medical term with any real significance, it is somehow fitting that a man who worked tirelessly his whole life should quite literally wear himself out.

Stoker was cremated and a small group of mourners watched as his ashes were placed in a stone casket. He had no epitaph.

After her husband's death, Florence Stoker became the executor of his estate. He left everything to her, though there was little to leave. She put up hundreds of his possessions for auction and made enough money to live on. She enjoyed her old age, remaining a beautiful and sought-after figure in London's society. She also guarded her husband's legacy fiercely.

In 1922, Florence heard that a German director was planning to make a film based on the novel *Dracula.* For a pittance, she joined the Society of Authors on her husband's behalf and immediately set about trying to stop the filmmakers from using his work. She waged a tenacious and remorseless campaign against the Germans, suing for copyright infringement, and then against the American company Universal that claimed to have purchased the rights to the story from the German filmmakers. Florence Stoker was successful in having most—but not all—copies of these unauthorized films destroyed and receiving financial compensation. When she died in 1935 at ninety-one, she left an estate worth half again as much as Stoker had left her originally.

Nosferatu, the 1922 film made in Germany, is considered to this day to be one of the best movies ever made. It was screened in London (despite Florence Stoker's protests) and has inspired many imitators. Perhaps the next most famous Dracula film was made in 1931, in Hollywood, starring Bela Lugosi. Many more Dracula movies would be made, including *Dracula's Daughter, Son of Dracula, Drakula Istanbulda, The Return of Dracula, The Curse of Dracula, The Horror of Dracula, Dracula—Prince of Darkness, Taste the Blood of Dracula, Dracula's Saga, In Search of Dracula, Bram Stoker's Dracula* (made twice, once in 1973 and again in 1992—the 1992 version won several Oscars), *Count Dracula: the True Story,* and a documentary called *Dracula: Fact or Fiction?* Stoker's novel, *The Lair of the White Worm*, would also be made into a movie.

Obituaries in England and Ireland praised Stoker both for his writing and for his dedication to the stage.

Bela Lugosi as Dracula, 1931.

A *New York Times* reporter wrote:

> [Stoker] wrote fluently and was eagerly interested in all the affairs of the world. Deep down in his nature there was a touch of Celtic mysticism. It sought expression in literary form, but his stories, though they were queer, were not of a memorable quality. His *Life of Irving*, however, is a noteworthy book. He had plenty of friends and enough enemies to indicate that his friendship was worth having. The embodiment of health and strength and geniality, it seems he died too young. He was only sixty-four years of age. Almost every one who knew him will say that he should have lived to be ninety, and kept a young heart in his old age.

Timeline

1847	Born in Clontarf, Ireland.
1854	Walks for the first time.
1863	Enrolls in Trinity College, Dublin.
1871	Becomes drama critic for the *Evening Mail;* graduates from Trinity.
1872	Sells first short story.
1877	Writes first book.
1878	Marries Florence Balcombe; becomes stage manager for Lyceum.
1886	Begins law studies.
1888	Seriously studies Romanian customs and history.
1890	Begins writing novel set in Romania.
1897	Publishes *Dracula*.
1912	Dies in England.

Sources

<hr>

CHAPTER ONE: Imagination Creates a World

p. 13, "This early weakness..." Bram Stoker, *Personal Reminiscences of Henry Irving* (London: Heineman, 1906), 32.

p. 15, "Give me now..." Walt Whitman, *Leaves of Grass* (New York: Aventine Press, 1931), 113.

CHAPTER TWO: The Theater Calls

p. 20-21, "Put it [the letter] in your fire..." Barbara Belford, *Bram Stoker* (New York: Alfred A. Knopf, 1996), 40.

p. 21, "I am ugly but strong..." Ibid., 42.

p. 23, "I wage a perpetual war..." Ibid.

p. 23, "You did well..." Ibid.

p. 26, "Irving's physical appearance..." Ibid., 72.

p. 27, "I became hysterical..." Daniel Farson, *The Man Who Wrote Dracula* (New York: St. Martin's Press, 1975), 30.

CHAPTER THREE: Art and Business Meet

p. 28, "exquisitely pretty girl..." Belford, *Bram Stoker,* 85.

p. 29, "complete guide to a clerk's..." Ibid.

p. 29, "a wild, fitful, irresolute..." Ibid., 80.

p. 30, "We understood each other's nature..." Ibid.

p. 30, "Will you give up…" Charles Osborne, ed., *The Bram Stoker Bedside Companion* (New York: Taplinger Publishing Co., 1973), 9.

p. 32, "Fortunately, for both myself…" Stoker, *Personal Reminiscences,* 62.

p. 36, "[Irving] gave one a…" Ibid.

CHAPTER FOUR: Travels Bring Successes and Trials

p. 37, "noble and sordid…" Jonathan Bate and Russell Jackson, eds., *Shakespeare: An Illustrated History* (Oxford; New York: Oxford University Press, 1996), 122.

p. 39, "I couldn't myself see…" Stoker, *Personal Reminiscences,* 166.

p. 41, "knew that the Giant…" Osborne, *Bedside Companion,* 48.

p. 41, "the things we do wrong…" Belford, *Bram Stoker,* 139.

p. 41, "a charming book…high and pure" Ibid., vi.

p. 48, "in three years, I judge…" Farson, *Man Who Wrote Dracula,* 74.

p. 48, "If I ever do it…" Belford, *Bram Stoker,* 165.

CHAPTER FIVE: Realism Demands Research

p. 49, "great shaggy masses…" Belford, *Bram Stoker,* 167.

p. 49, "a breath of good, healthy…" Ibid., 168.

p. 50, "[it is] deplorable…" Farson, *Man Who Wrote Dracula,* 72.

p. 52, "we are bound…" Ibid., 78.

p. 53, "[in this play] two iron plates…" Stoker, *Personal Reminisences,* 176.

p. 53-54, "And sitting on the head…" Osborne, *Bedside Companion,* 127.

p. 55, "[clouds] so dank and damp…" Belford,*Bram Stoker,* 194.

p. 55, "about a hundred lines in all…" Ibid., 198.

CHAPTER SIX: Writing Competes with the Theater

p. 59, "I often say to…" Nina Auerbach, *Ellen Terry: Player in Her Time* (New York: W.W. Norton & Co., 1987), 89.

p. 60, "indolent charm…companions," Emily Gerard, *The Land Beyond the Forest* (New York: Haper & Bros., 1888), 1.

p. 60, "it would almost seem…" Ibid.

p. 61, "In very obstinate cases…" Ibid., 185.

p. 63, "Dracula in Wallachian…" Raymond McNally and Radu Florescu, *In Search of Dracula* (Boston: Houghton Mifflin Company, 1994), 49.

p. 63-64, "the *penangula* takes possession…," Ibid., 192.

p. 64, "I sat next to him…dagger," Belford, *Bram Stoker,* 238.

p. 68, "The red glare of the sunset…" Bram Stoker, *Miss Betty,* (London: New English Library), 100.

CHAPTER SEVEN: Count Dracula Casts His Spell

p. 70, "cool it with dragoon's blood…" Stoker, *Personal Reminiscences,* 137.

p. 71, "All shall be well…" Ibid.

p. 71, "the journey—wolves howl…" Exhibition Catalogue of Rosenbach Museum & Library, 29.

p. 71, "I really think…" Farson, *Man Who Wrote Dracula,* 62.

p. 72, "a mass that in the gloom…" Osborne, *Bedside Companion,* 222.

p. 73, "The history of the…" Stoker, *Personal Reminiscences,* 266-67.

p. 74, "Aug. 11 bat outside…" McNally, *In Search of Dracula,* 109.

p. 77, "suddenly I felt a hand…" Mary Shelley, et al., *Frankenstein, Dracula, Mr. Jekyll and Mr. Hyde* (NAL Dutton: New York, 1978), 34.

p. 78, "He disgusted me…" Ibid., 78.

p. 78, "You may go anywhere…" Ibid., 35.

CHAPTER EIGHT: A Writing Career Flourishes

p. 79, "Dreadful!" Rosenbach catalogue, 31.

p. 80, "the book is necessarily full…" Ibid., 33.

p. 80, "My dear, it is splendid…" Ibid.

p. 80, "reads at times..." Rosenbach catalogue, 33.

p. 82, "weird, powerful and horrible..." Osborne, *Bedside Companion,* 11.

p. 82, "Trees are trees..." Belford, *Bram Stoker,* 220.

p. 85,"pretty much the same..." Ibid., 282.

p. 86, "Splash! My feet had given way..." Osborne, *Bedside Companion,* 92.

p. 88, "at times we rolled..." Belford, *Bram Stoker,* 286.

p. 88, "a great shambling, good-natured..." Ibid., 288.

CHAPTER NINE: Goodbyes

p. 94, "unclean...foully-conceived novel," Belford, *Bram Stoker,* 312.

p. 95, "A number of books..." Osborne, *Bedside Companion,* 13.

p. 97, "imposters in one shape..." Phyllis Roth, *Bram Stoker* (Boston: Twayne Publishers, 1982), 129.

p. 97, "I can now stand..." Belford, 315.

p. 101, "[Stoker] wrote fluently and was..." *New York Times,* (April 23, 1912), 12.

Bibliography

Auerbach, Nina. *Ellen Terry: Player in Her Time.* New York: W.W. Norton & Company, 1987.

Belford, Barbara. *Bram Stoker: The Biography of the Author of Dracula.* New York: Alfred A. Knopf, 1996.

Farson, Daniel. *The Man Who Wrote Dracula.* New York: St. Martin's Press, 1975.

Gerard, Emily. *The Land Beyond the Forest: Facts, Figures, and Fancies.* New York: Harper & Brothers, 1888.

Kenyon, Fred C. *Hall Caine: The Man and the Novelist.* New York: Haskell House Publisher, Ltd., 1974.

Leatherdale, Clive. *The Origins of Dracula.* London: William Kimber, 1987.

McNally, Raymond and Radu Florescu. *In Search of Dracula.* Boston: Houghton Mifflin Company, 1994.

Melton, J. Gordon. *The Vampire Book: The Encyclopedia of the Undead.* Detroit: Gale Research, Inc., 1994.

Osborne, Charles, ed. *The Bram Stoker Bedside Companion.* New York: Taplinger Publishing Company, 1973.

Rosenbach Museum & Library catalogue for the Centennial Exhibition of *Dracula.* Philadelphia, 1997.

Roth, Phyllis. *Bram Stoker*. Boston: Twayne Publishers, 1982.

Stoker, Bram. *Famous Imposters*. New York: Sturgis & Walton Co., 1910.

———. *Famous Imposters*. New York: Sturgis & Walton Co., 1910.

———. *Lair of the White Worm*. London: Rider, 1911.

———. *Miss Betty*. London: New English Library, no date given.

———. *The Mystery of the Sea*. New York: Doubleday, 1902.

———. *Personal Reminisces of Henry Irving*, 2 vols. London: Heinemann, 1906.

———. *Under the Sunset*. Hollywood: Newcastle Publishing Company, Inc., 1978.

Whitman, Walt. *Leaves of Grass*. New York: Aventine Press, 1931.

Wolf, Leonard. *The Essential Dracula*. New York: A Byron Preiss Book, 1975.

Woodham-Smith, Cecil. *The Great Hunger*. New York: Harper & Row, 1962.

Index